# Nes

Written by Jo Windsor

This nest is
in the tree.

nest

This nest is
on the ground.

nest

This nest is
on the rocks.

nest

This nest is
in the ground.

nest

This nest is
on the chimney.

nest

This nest is
in the grass.

nest

# Index

nests in

    the grass  . . . . 12-13

    the ground  . . . . .8-9

    the tree  . . . . . . . 2-3

nests on

    the chimney . . 10-11

    the ground  . . . . .4-5

    the rocks  . . . . . . 6-7

# Guide Notes

**Title: Nesting Places**
**Stage:** Emergent – Magenta

**Genre:** Nonfiction (Expository)
**Approach:** Guided Reading
**Processes:** Thinking Critically, Exploring Language, Processing Information
**Written and Visual Focus:** Photographs (static images), Index, Labels

## FORMING THE FOUNDATION

Tell the children that this book is about places where birds make their nests.
Talk to them about what is on the front cover. Read the title and the author.
Focus the children's attention on the index and talk about the places that are in the book.
"Walk" through the book, focusing on the photographs and talk about the birds and the different places they have used to build their nests.

**Read the text together.**

## THINKING CRITICALLY

(sample questions)

**After the reading**
- What might happen if the bird could not make a nest?
- Why do you think some birds make nests on the ground?

## EXPLORING LANGUAGE

(ideas for selection)

**Terminology**
Title, cover, author, photographs

**Vocabulary**
**Interest words:** nest, tree, ground, rocks, chimney, grass
**High-frequency words:** this, is, in, the, on
**Positional words:** in, on